Welcome to
BLETCHLEYPARK

Bletchley Park has global significance. It is where the World War Two Codebreakers broke seemingly impenetrable codes and ciphers, and it is where the world's first electronic computers were installed and operated.

The intelligence produced here contributed to all theatres of World War Two. Bletchley Park pioneered co-operation with other intelligence services including France, Poland and the United States. The techniques developed here played a major role in the Cold War and, in many cases, remain highly relevant today.

The site is a portal into the information age in which we live, as unique data-processing machines were developed to help speed up the codebreaking effort.

Bletchley History 1938 to now

In 1938 the British Government bought part of the then much larger Bletchley Park estate to house the most secret codebreaking and intelligence efforts of the Government Code and Cypher School (GC&CS) in a quiet rural location, easily reached from London, Cambridge and Oxford. It was fully expected that in a future war London would come under heavy air attack. Over the next few months, as war loomed, the first wooden huts were built and communications channels were established. GC&CS finally moved from London in August 1939.

Early in the war the Bletchley Park operation centred on the work of a small group of experts. It went on to pioneer the application of close inter-service liaison and production line methods to the key stages of the process – collection, codebreaking, evaluation and dissemination.

German Air Force and Army Enigma settings were changed daily at midnight and even before the first Enigma ciphers were broken in early 1940, Cambridge mathematician Gordon Welchman realised GC&CS would need a structured, factory-like process to ensure the daily settings were broken as efficiently as possible. In April 1940, after the invasion of Norway, a round-the-clock shift system was introduced.

From May 1940 there was a massive increase in the volume and complexity of traffic, as the theatre of war widened. The so-called Phoney War ended with the German invasion of Denmark and Norway in April 1940. A new Enigma key (the machine's setting) was introduced and it took the Codebreakers in Hut 6 six days to break it. This break into the new key told the Allies every move the German Army was making, and was about to make.

The Codebreakers' arrival at Bletchley Park

By early 1943 Bletchley Park had developed from a small community of specialist cryptanalysts into a vast and complex global signals intelligence factory. It hit its peak in early 1945, when around ten thousand people worked at Bletchley and its associated outstations. The contributions of Bletchley Park's Codebreakers to the outcome of World War Two are now globally recognised. They include:

- Location of the German 'U-Boat' submarines in the Battle of the Atlantic
- Providing early warning of German air attacks on British cities
- Production of intelligence to support the Mediterranean and North African campaigns
- Contributing to the success of Operation Overlord through the work of a number of sections at Bletchley Park in breaking German High Command, military and Secret Service communications, as well as Japanese diplomatic messages
- Helping to identify new weapons including German V weapons, jet aircraft, atomic research and new U-Boats
- Analysis of the effect of the war on the German economy
- Breaking Japanese codes and producing intelligence that helped secure the successful outcome of the war in the Pacific

After the war, GC&CS became Government Communications Headquarters (GCHQ) and it left Bletchley Park in 1946. The site was used as a training school for the Control Commission which governed post-war Germany, then a teacher training college, and later a training centre for the Civil Aviation Authority and the GPO, which became British Telecom. In 1992 a group of local historians saved the site from developers' bulldozers and the Bletchley Park Trust was formed to preserve the site for the nation.

The same view of the Mansion today

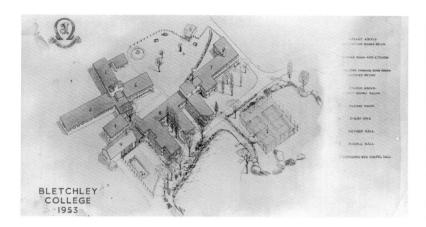

Bletchley Park in 1953

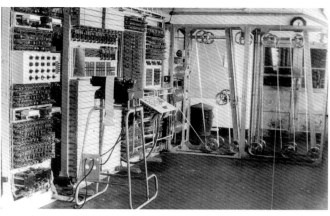

Colossus, the world's first electronic digital computer

Aerial view, 1966

Above: Bombe machine under construction

Right: Bletchley Park in 2003

Breaking Enigma

The standard three-rotor Enigma was capable of being set to approximately 159,000,000,000,000,000,000 possible combinations. Further versions were developed during the war, several with four rotors, including the German Naval M4, which, along with a new weather key, locked the Codebreakers out of Naval Enigma for ten months during 1942.

Left: Three-rotor Enigma

Above right: Enigma rotors

Above: Enigma rotors with numbered rings (German Army or Air Force)

The Enigma used rotors to scramble messages into unintelligible cipher text. The German military adapted an early commercial version, marketed to the banking industry, and believed it to be impenetrable. Each one of the machine's billions of possible combinations generated completely different cipher text. Finding those settings – most of which were reset at midnight every day – was the challenge faced by the Codebreakers.

Before World War Two, work was being undertaken in a number of countries to break Enigma. In July 1939, aware that Poland would soon be invaded, the Poles shared the work of their mathematicians who had worked on Enigma with the British and the French. By this time the Germans were changing most of the Enigma settings daily and the first British wartime breaks into the daily-changing Enigma code took place at Bletchley Park in January 1940.

The number of different possible settings for the Enigma machine are staggering. Each rotor could be set to any one of 26 different ring settings. Then the plug board could be set in a vast number of different ways. The settings were also different for the Army, Air Force, Navy and Secret Service, and most were changed daily. The main task of the Codebreakers was to deduce the daily Enigma settings, so the Bombe machine became vital.

Above: Bombe Room chart

Top left: Bombe drum

Top right: Rows of drums on the Bombe

The Bombe machine was developed by Alan Turing and Gordon Welchman to speed up the breaking of Enigma, so that messages were still operationally relevant. It was inspired by the 'Bomba', an earlier machine designed by the Polish Cypher Bureau. The Bombe helped to deduce the day's Enigma settings, of both the rotors and the plug board, by eliminating the many incorrect possibilities.

The Codebreakers created a menu for the wiring at the back of the Bombe based on a hypothesis, known as a 'crib', of part of the original message. Cribs were often derived from regular appearances in deciphered messages of stock phrases, such as 'message number' or 'nothing significant to report'.

Above: Bombe wiring

Left: Enigma machine in use in General Heinz Guderian's command vehicle in France, May 1940

The drums on the Bombe each represented a rotor on the Enigma. The Bombe had 108 drums, each vertical set of three representing an Enigma machine. The menu told the operators how to connect the drums with plug leads at the back of the machine as well as their starting positions. The drums were then driven through all 17,576 positions, which took around twelve minutes.

If at one or more of the 17,576 positions the Bombe detected that the logic of the menu was satisfied, it would slow down and stop, supplying the Codebreakers with possible settings of the Enigma machine. The Codebreakers would check those settings on a checking machine and, utilising the intercepted message header, deduce the Enigma settings of the day. They would then apply those settings to a modified Typex machine – the British equivalent to Enigma – and type the enciphered message. If they'd got it right, plain German text came out, in groups of five letters. All of that day's intercepted messages on that network could then be deciphered using the Typex, and the Bombe could start on the settings of another network.

The Bombe sped up the process but a great deal of deduction was required both before and after the machine was run. Breaking into the new Enigma settings was a huge intellectual feat, which the Codebreakers achieved most days, usually in the middle of the night.

Right: Part of the keyboard of a teleprinter

Below: British cipher machine, Typex

Breaking Lorenz

Even more complex than the Enigma was the Lorenz cipher machine. It was used by Hitler himself, the High Command and German Army Field Marshals. It was much bigger and heavier than the Enigma and had twelve wheels. The Codebreakers called the machine Tunny and the coded messages Fish. Cracking Lorenz, like Enigma, relied on determining the starting position of the wheels.

Lorenz used the international teleprinter code, in which each letter of the alphabet was represented by a series of five electrical impulses. Extra letters were generated by the wheels and added to the original text. Five of the twelve wheels followed a regular movement pattern

Above: Inside the Lorenz attachment

Left: Lorenz cipher attachment

and two wheels dictated the movement pattern of the other five. To decipher a message, the receiving Lorenz added the same obscuring letters.

The enciphered message was fed directly into a radio transmitter, which transmitted it to a distant receiving station. Here it was fed straight into a Lorenz machine. Both machines had to be set exactly the same way.

The Germans began using the Lorenz machine in the second half of 1940. The teleprinter signals were intercepted but the Codebreakers knew nothing about the machine being used to encipher them. Then one German operator made a horrendous mistake.

The mechanism of a Lorenz attachment

In August 1941 a long message was sent between Athens and Vienna. The operator transmitted a clear twelve-letter indicator which told the receiving operator the exact wheel start positions. He entered all 4,000 characters only to be told by the receiving operator that he hadn't got it. Assuming the system was unbreakable, the operator used the same settings and, because it was standard procedure, sent the indicator again. This time he abbreviated a number of words to save time.

The combination of the use of the same indicator and the abbreviations gave Bletchley's chief cryptanalyst John Tiltman a way in. It took Tiltman ten days but he recovered both German messages in full, thanks to the operator's mistake.

Bill Tutte, a Cambridge chemistry graduate, deduced through mathematical analysis how the Lorenz machine worked without ever

having seen one. A new section was set up to capitalise on Tiltman's and Tutte's achievements, called The Testery after its leader Ralph Tester, a former accountant who had lived and worked in Germany.

From mid-1942, intercepted Lorenz messages were punched on to teleprinter tape and sent via both teleprinter and dispatch rider to The Testery. There they were deciphered from gibberish to German.

By 1943 the Germans had introduced complications which made it virtually impossible to break Lorenz by hand – or brain – alone. The first machine designed by Max Newman and his team in The Newmanry was christened Heath Robinson, after the cartoon designer of fantastic contraptions. It worked, but was slow and unreliable, so Max Newman called upon Tommy Flowers, a brilliant Post Office electronics engineer. Flowers designed Colossus, the

Left: Colossus in operation, 1944

Above: Thyratron valves in a Colossus machine

Above right: Heath Robinson was slow and unreliable

Right: Colossus tape drive pulley

world's first practical electronic digital and information processing machine – the forerunner of the modern computer. It would eventually use 2,500 thermionic valves (vacuum tubes) and the first Colossus machine arrived at Bletchley in January 1944.

Colossus could read paper tape at 5,000 characters per second, the paper tape in its wheels travelling at 30 miles per hour. This meant that

the huge amount of mathematical work that needed to be done to break Lorenz could be carried out in hours, rather than weeks.

The first Colossus was joined by a second in June 1944, and was working in time for Eisenhower and Montgomery to be sure that Hitler had swallowed the deception plan prior to D-Day on 6 June 1944. There were eventually ten working Colossi at Bletchley Park.

Other Codes and Ciphers

Bletchley Park did not only break into Enigma and Lorenz. The Codebreakers also cracked a number of other ciphers being used by enemy forces during World War Two.

The Hagelin C38 for example, a Swedish machine, was introduced in 1938 and used by the Italian Navy, the US Navy and Army and the Royal Navy. The Italian system was broken by Bletchley Park, giving details of the convoys taking German troops and supplies to North Africa.

Above: Inside the Hagelin C38

Left: Hagelin C38 cipher machine

Significant effort went into breaking Japanese codes too. Around 55 different systems were used during the course of World War Two. Most were numeric but some lower-grade messages were encoded using letter-based ciphers. The sheer size of the Pacific helped the Allies as it meant, for much of the war, keys and codebooks were rarely replaced because it was impractical to send out new ones too often, over such great distances. So once the Allies broke into a code, they had a longer window than with other cipher systems before it was changed.

There were other cipher systems which didn't even involve machines. A book cipher codenamed Barbara is an example of paper-based systems. It was based on a double transposition cipher and was used by Germany to send weather reports. John Tiltman broke into this system in March 1940.

Left: The SG-41, intended to replace Enigma. It was never broken but production problems and the end of the war prevented it from being successfully deployed

Below: Relays in a Sturgeon machine

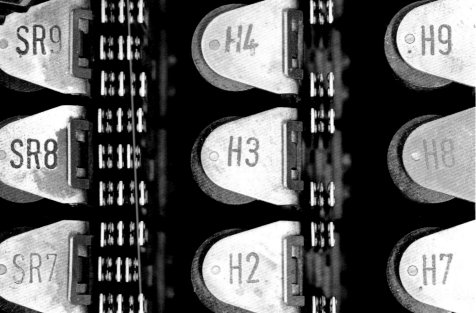

The Development of the Bletchley Park site

Bletchley Park is unique. It housed a collection of brilliant minds tasked with codebreaking during World War Two, thereby altering the course of history.

The surviving fabric of Bletchley Park shows every stage of the advances made in cryptographic, computing and intelligence processes. War work at Bletchley Park began in the Mansion, then expanded into hastily built timber huts and, later, brick, steel and concrete blocks, most of which still stand today.

The decision to give the codebreaking operation the resources it needed to expand was given urgency by Winston Churchill himself in 1941, when he encouraged his Chiefs of Staff to 'Action this Day' requests from Bletchley. This urgency reflected the pressures of total war. The construction of the blocks marked the Allies' transition from defensive to offensive military operations, including the bomber offensive, the break-out from North Africa and preparations for the invasion of Europe.

Above: Bletchley Park, July 1940

Right: View from the Mansion in 1945

Above: View from Hut 2

Right: Map showing the development of Bletchley Park 1939-45, courtesy of English Heritage

The development of the huts and blocks, from the original nucleus centred on the Mansion and Stableyard, shows how codebreaking was industrialised and is a testament to the development of information technology. Bletchley Park is now a unique surviving example of a country house and park adapted for wartime use, and typifies developments at hundreds of country homes requisitioned for use during World War Two.

N

1939
1940
1941
1942
1943
1944

Figure 14.4.1
Plan showing construction phases
1939 - 1945
(Based on 1943 site plan)
(c English Heritage)

ENGLISH HERITAGE

The Mansion

The Mansion dates back to the late 1870s. It was bought, along with the surrounding estate, in 1883 by Sir Herbert Leon, a wealthy stockbroker.

During World War Two, the Mansion served as the headquarters and recreational building. The major codebreaking sections initially worked on the ground floor, before the expansion into the Huts. The main cafeteria was housed in the Dining Room until April 1942. The Mansion also housed the offices of senior staff such as John Tiltman, head of the Military Section, Commander Alastair Denniston, head of GC&CS until 1942, and Commander Edward Travis, head from 1942 and the first post-war head of GCHQ.

The first telephone exchange was in the Billiard Room.

The Mansion is open to visitors.

Denniston made clear his intention to provide facilities for relaxation from the mental stresses of work. The first meeting of the Joint Committee of Control, which ran the internal organisation of Bletchley Park from 1941 to 1942, issued a memo which read:

'In my view we have reached a stage in the development of BP when our main and most serious drawback to efficiency and the sense of good feeling on which efficiency must depend, is not the absence of adequate space to work, but the absence of any place at all to play ... somewhere where all can have their cup of coffee and cigarette without condemning the vast majority, seniors and juniors alike, to stand cheek by jowl like sardines in a tin.'

The Mansion before World War Two

At work in the Library, circa 1939/40

Left: The Mansion

Below: Griffins guard the Mansion entrance

Above: The Library, dressed as it looked during World War Two

Stableyard

During World War Two there were three cottages on the north side of the Stableyard, the Apple and Pear Store on the south side, which later became known as the Bungalow, and the West Range, used for vehicles and carrier pigeons which received messages from occupied Europe.

Codebreakers including Alan Turing and Dilly Knox worked in the Cottages from September 1939. The first breaks into daily-changing German Enigma were made here. This success was kept secret even within Bletchley Park. The breaking of the German Secret Service (Abwehr) codes by Dilly Knox and his team, Illicit Signals Knox (ISK), in December 1941 supported the Double Cross operation prior to D-Day.

- The break into Italian Enigma that underpinned victory in the naval Battle of Matapan, off Crete in March 1941, was achieved in the Cottages
- Alan Turing and Gordon Welchman developed ideas for the first electromechanical Bombe in the Bungalow

Codenamed Operation Fortitude South, the Double Cross operation led the Germans to believe that the Allied plan to invade Normandy was actually a diversion from the true target, the Pas de Calais. This allowed the Allies to land at Normandy while the Germans laid in

The Garages in wartime

The Garages today

fortified wait in Calais. Abwehr Enigma messages broken in the Cottage made it clear that Germany had swallowed the deception whole.

The Cottages were also home to the Head of Works Services, Mr Budd and his family – including twin daughters who were six years old when they arrived at Bletchley Park. The Budds were one of only two families who lived on site.

Today in the Stableyard the Polish Memorial commemorates the achievements of the three mathematicians – Marian Rejewski, Henryk Zygalski and Jerzy Różycki – who broke Enigma using mathematical methods in 1933 and handed their work on Enigma to the British in 1939, helping to advance the codebreaking efforts of the Allies.

The Cottages

Beyond the Garages is the gate where most of the dispatch riders arrived. As many as forty riders delivered up to 3,000 messages a day.

The wartime Garages are open for visitors; however, the other buildings in the Stableyard can be viewed from the outside but are closed to the public.

The Clock Tower in wartime

The restored Clock Tower

The Polish Memorial

Hut 1

Hut 1 was one of the first to be built. Its initial purpose was to house the MI6 wireless transmission station which was originally in the Mansion's water tower. Aerials were strung from the Mansion to the tall trees at the front.

The first Bombe machine, Victory, was tested in Hut 1 in early 1940, in what was then a sick bay. Later in the war Hut 1 became the Transport Office. A mere handful of the Codebreakers lived on site, the rest being billeted around Bletchley and the surrounding countryside and having to get to and from the site in large numbers for the three eight-hour shifts each day and night.

Hut 1 is not yet open to visitors.

Hut 1

Hut 1 with remnants of wartime bomb blast walls

Left to right: Huts 3, 6 and 1

Huts 2 & 9

Hut 2 was one of the first wooden huts to be completed and ready for use, in August 1939. It was located just to the north of the front of the Mansion and provided a home for a number of recreational activities. It issued cups of tea, sandwiches and sold luncheon vouchers throughout the war, and from 25 February 1943 was also permitted to sell beer over lunch and at tea times. Hut 2 also housed the lending library run by a Mrs Vivian until May 1942. The library was then moved from Hut 2, along with the BP Recreational Club, to the Mansion. From mid-1942 Hut 2 was used two evenings a week for Naval Section language courses (one evening for German, one evening for Italian). By June 1944 it was being used as a Casualty Reception Station during 'BP in danger' ARP exercises. Hut 2 was eventually demolished in the 1980s to make way for a car park.

Hut 9 is believed to be the original Hut 3, used for Japanese and Italian overflow work. It was renamed Hut 9 in early 1940 and used for a number of activities until early 1942, when it became Bletchley Park's main administration hut.

In November 2013, whilst restoration of the wartime landscape was underway with the removal of post-war car parks, archaeological work was undertaken and the footings of Huts 2 and 9 were discovered. These footings have been carefully conserved and the footprints of the two huts, including Hut 9's later extension, marked out for visitors to see.

Right: Hut 2 in the 1970s between the Mansion and Hut 9

Hut 3

Once German Army and Air Force Enigma messages had been deciphered in Hut 6, they were passed next door to Hut 3 for translation and analysis. It was also the main reporting centre for enciphered teleprinter messages, named Fish by the Codebreakers, decrypted in The Testery and Newmanry in Block F.

The translators in Hut 3 had to make German military language, strictly formatted and littered with jargon, read like a credible report from a fake spy. Most recipients were never told that a message had come from Bletchley Park, nor that it was based on intercept.

The writer and poet FL Lucas, who worked in Hut 3, said 'It was not a matter of receiving straightforward messages and translating them: it was always a matter of receiving material which was nearly always more or less imperfect, often incomplete, rarely intelligible with ease, and at its worst totally meaningless to even the best German scholar.'

Inside Hut 3

Hut 3 today with reinstated blast walls

As the importance of the work carried out in the huts grew, so did the number of staff needed. By 1942 Hut 3 activity was no longer housed in a single wooden structure but in a whole range of locations and buildings around Bletchley Park. This is also true of the other huts.

Hut 3 has been restored to its wartime condition and is open to visitors.

Chris Hayes, one of the young women recruited to work at Bletchley Park, recalled 'I was told to report to Bletchley railway station, and walk up to the Main House for an interview. I was not told the nature of the work before I got there, and have kept quiet about it for the past fifty years! I was sent to Hut 3, and my younger sister Lola Horan joined me at Bletchley Park six months later and was sent to Hut 6.'

Hut 3 corridor

Inside Hut 3

Hut 4

Before the arrival of GC&CS, the Library in the Mansion looked out over a beautiful rose garden.

Originally housing the German Air Force and Naval Sections, from mid-1940 the main function of this hut was translating and analysing German naval Enigma messages deciphered by Hut 8. These two huts provided crucial day-to-day intelligence in the desperate battles between the Allied convoys and the U-Boats which were determined to cut Britain's vitally important supply lines across the Atlantic.

Hut 4 viewed through the Mansion windows

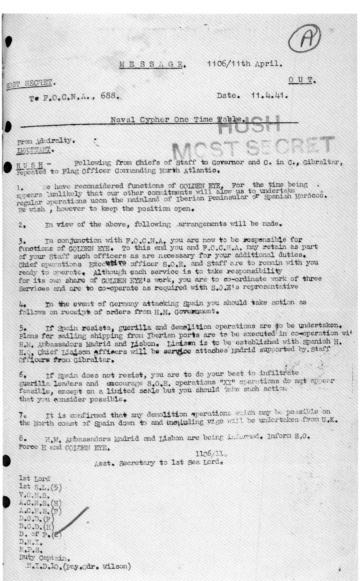

'Most Secret' later became 'Top Secret'

Early in the war, relations between the Naval Section in Hut 4 and the Admiralty were strained, as many in Naval Intelligence were unconvinced of the reliability of information emerging from Bletchley Park. But in 1941 the Enigma system being used by the U-Boats, codenamed Dolphin, was broken thanks to a combination of repetitive weather transmissions and a captured book of Enigma keys. This was a major breakthrough. Dolphin was broken and then read every day until the end of the war.

Today Hut 4 houses the café.

Above right: Children's Play Area outside Hut 4

Right: Hut 4 now houses the café

Hut 6

Hut 6 was built in January 1940 for the deciphering of Enigma messages from the German Army and Air Force. Initially the work was conducted with help from perforated sheets which were known as Zygalski sheets after the Polish Codebreaker who invented them. The Bletchley Park Codebreakers referred to these as Netz and they were used to help deduce part of each Enigma key. Later efforts were assisted by the Bombe machines initially located in Huts 11 and 11A.

Once the day's Enigma settings had been partially established with help from the Bombes, the information was sent back to Hut 6 where it was used to complete the discovery of the Enigma settings. Deciphered messages were then passed to Hut 3 for translation and analysis.

A specially built chute was created to send deciphered messages securely to Hut 3. It was not as high-tech as many of Bletchley Park's wartime innovations; a broom handle was used to convey a basket containing messages between the two huts. There were complaints about the draught coming in from the chute and a carpenter was called in to install flaps at either end. This put an end to the method of alerting the other hut that a message was coming – calling out – and the sender moved on to banging the chute with the broom handle instead.

Hut 6 has been restored to its wartime condition and is open to visitors.

Right: The Hut 6 Machine Room was set up to work out the daily Enigma keys by hand. When it moved from the small wooden hut to Block D, its main task was to produce instructions for the women who set up the Bombe machines and then tested possible key settings passed to them by the Bombe operators

Above left: The Hut 6 Control Room had a wide-ranging role. When it moved from the small wooden hut to Block D, its focus was on organising and maintaining relations between Hut 6 and the intercept stations, offering a continuous service to direct cover and assist interception

Above: Hut 6 today

Above right: Projections on the walls authentically capture the World War Two ambience

Right: Hut 6, wartime scene of Army and Air Force codebreaking

Hut 8

Hut 8 was built in January 1940 for the deciphering of raw material from the Navy. The first break into naval Enigma – codenamed Dolphin – early in 1941 had a significant impact on the Battle of the Atlantic. Information deciphered in Hut 8 helped to reduce the destruction wrought by the U-Boats in the Atlantic.

Under its heads Alan Turing and then Hugh Alexander Hut 8, like Hut 6, also became a major driving force in the development of analytical machines to speed up the deciphering process.

Even after the naval Enigma operation moved to Block D it was still called Hut 8. The old hut was renamed Hut 18. During the D-Day landings intercept operators were based there to ensure swift warning of any German naval attacks.

Hut 8 today

Naval Enigma was broken in Hut 8

Hut 8 at the end of the war

Alan Turing used his office in Hut 8 to write academic papers in his spare time, some of which are now on show in the Block B Turing Exhibition.

In Hut 8 visitors can see Alan Turing's office and test their codebreaking skills in the Brilliant Minds Exhibition.

Above and right: Visitors enjoy the interactive displays in Hut 8

Huts 11 & 11A

Hut 11 was built to house the Bombe machines developed by Alan Turing and Gordon Welchman to speed up the daily search for the Enigma cipher keys used by the German Army, Air Force, Navy and Secret Service. It replaced a smaller, wooden hut, the concrete structure providing the protection needed for such precious machines.

Bombes were eventually mass-produced. These two buildings at Bletchley Park were given over to housing them initially, but there were far more at outstations in local villages and as far away as Eastcote and Stanmore on the outskirts of London. Even more were produced and operated in the United States. Hut 11A became the main control centre for all Bombes in the UK.

Hut 11A was built in March 1942, as more Bombes were needed and made, and it also became a training centre for the Women's Royal Naval Service – WRNS, known as 'Wrens' – who operated the machines and nicknamed this hot and noisy hut the 'Hell Hole'.

Wrens operated the Bombe machines

Hut 11

The first Newmanry was established here in 1943, under Max Newman. This section developed machines to help decipher German teleprinter codes. These two huts provided a highly secure environment for the crucial machines.

Hut 11 has been restored to its wartime layout and now tells the story through the eyes of the people who worked there. Hut 11A will also be brought back to life and opened to the public in due course.

A typical Bombe room with the WRNS operators

Inside Hut 11 today

Hut 12

Hut 12 started as an annex to Hut 3, and later became part of Hut 4's naval Enigma operation. It then housed the Intelligence Exchange, with cryptanalyst Nigel de Grey at the helm.

Ian Fleming, the James Bond creator, worked for Naval Intelligence and was responsible for liaising with Bletchley Park. He planned an operation to capture a naval Enigma machine, Operation Ruthless, which never came to fruition, but the qualities he described in the operative it would need were remarkably similar to the 007 character he later created.

Above: Hut 12

By April 1943 Hut 12 was known as the Education Hut, used for chamber music classes and orchestral evenings held by the BP Musical Society.

Today Hut 12 is open to the public.

The wartime BP Musical Society who would have used Hut 12 to rehearse

A
CONCERT OF
ENGLISH MUSIC
BY THE
B.P. MUSICAL SOCIETY
(Conductor - HERBERT MURRILL)
IN THE
Assembly Hall, Wilton Avenue,
FRIDAY, SEPT. 8th,
SATURDAY, SEPT. 9th,
MONDAY, SEPT. 11th,
TUESDAY, SEPT. 12th,
at 8 p.m. sharp.

Programme : Sixpence.

All Proceeds to
The Sailors', Soldiers' and Airmens' Families Association.

Left: Creativity thrived at Bletchley Park

Block A

In March 1941 a decision was made which would alter the landscape and layout of Bletchley Park forever. The codebreaking factory had outgrown the Mansion, Cottages and wooden huts, and a programme of building more permanent brick and concrete blocks was begun.

The first of these was Block A. There was still a significant threat of air attack so Blocks A and B, which were built at the same time, were bomb-proofed and shrouded by trees, more being planted to break up shadows thrown by the moon.

Blocks A and B were meant to house all three sections, Naval, Air and Army. Staff working on the translation and analysis of naval Enigma messages initially moved to Block A from Hut 4 in August 1942, but by mid-1943 the Naval section had taken over the building, such was the volume of messages it was decoding. Huge charts of the Atlantic covered the walls.

Today much of Block A houses commercial offices and is not open to the public.

Above: Steel, brick and concrete blocks were built from 1941

Left: Some blocks were reinforced against bomb blasts

Block B

Block B was built along with Block A, as Bletchley Park grew into a mechanised codebreaking factory. Block B was hardened, like Block A, in case of attack. In mid-September 1942 the remainder of the staff working on the translation and analysis of naval Enigma messages moved here from Hut 4.

Today, Block B houses various exhibitions and galleries relating to wartime Bletchley Park, including The Life and Works of Alan Turing, the largest public display of Enigma Machines in the world, and an exhibition about the breaking of the Lorenz cipher – Hitler's 'Unbreakable' Cipher Machine.

Block B and the Public Memorial to the Veterans of Bletchley Park and its Outstations

Display of equipment used for wireless interception in Block B

Display of Enigma Machines in Block B

The Turing Exhibition in Block B

The slate Turing statue in Block B

In 1941 the German Navy introduced a fourth rotor to the Enigma machines being used by the U-Boats. This vastly increased the number of possible settings. Shaun Wylie, head of the Hut 8 Crib Section, said, 'We knew it was coming. But it was a grim time. We realised that our work meant lives and it ceased to be fun.'

The Lorenz machine on display in Block B

Block C

Block C was the home of the Freebornery (named after the man in charge, Frederic Freeborn). This was where Hollerith punch-card machines/tabulating machinery, a form of mechanical data-processor that preceded the computer, carried out rapid analysis of enemy codes and cipher systems cutting the time it took to break them. Significant details from messages were recorded on punch cards and clerks, mainly women, ran the cards through the machines to find details and patterns that might help the Codebreakers. At its peak, two million cards per week were being used.

This was originally housed in Hut 7, but in November 1942 it moved to the new, soundproofed, brick-built Block C. Different machines were used for punching the cards, sorting and collating, and they varied in size from similar to a typewriter up to a piano. Although it was a tried and tested technology, the machines were continually adapted in conditions of absolute secrecy.

Block C is now the Visitor Centre.

Cabinets holding Hollerith punch cards in Block C

Hollerith machines in Block C during World War Two

Block C today. This space now houses the coffee shop seating area

The Visitor Centre in Block C

The level of secrecy the Codebreakers worked under is sometimes difficult to imagine in the information age we live in today. Bletchley Park provided the Allies with an unprecedented wealth of intelligence on the enemy's movements and plans. This intelligence was given the codename ULTRA. Only a handful of top commanders were privileged to receive it, but were forbidden to act upon it until the Germans had been deceived into thinking the information could have come from another source. The need-to-know principle was paramount, even at Bletchley Park itself. Few staff knew the whole story or even which other sections existed besides their own, much less what they all did.

Visitors enjoy the Introductory Exhibition in Block C

Block D

Block D was built for secrecy, both inside and out. Its layout – with spurs off a corridor – was designed to keep different departments separate, so that staff knew only what they needed to. Around a thousand people worked here and a pneumatic tube system and conveyor belt were installed to speed up communication.

One spur housed the American contingent. The number of United States personnel connected to Bletchley Park eventually reached around 230. It was here that the 'special relationship', initiated politically by Winston Churchill and President Roosevelt, was firmly cemented into British-United States affairs.

When Block D opened, all the staff working in Huts 3, 6 and 8 moved in and it became the heart of Bletchley Park's operation to break Enigma messages. It also housed the Hut 6 traffic analysis section known as SIXTA, which helped build a picture of the German order of battle. Much intelligence planning and decoding for the Normandy invasion took place within these walls.

Above: Sovex convey system in Block D

Block D is currently derelict, but the Bletchley Park Trust has long-term plans for its restoration.

One key figure in the D-Day deception, which led Hitler to believe the Normandy landings were a diversionary tactic to draw his troops away from the real target, the Pas de Calais, was a Spanish spy named Garbo. He was a double agent, who invented a network of no less than 27 fictitious spies, claiming expenses for them all from Germany. Bletchley Park was able to read messages sent between the German Secret Service (Abwehr) and Garbo's controller in Spain, which showed that the Abwehr fully believed the deception.

The imposing entrance to Block D

Block E

Block E was the hub of outward communication from Bletchley Park. Messages were re-enciphered using Typex machines and transmitted to Allied headquarters.

Special Communication Units (SCUs) passed the highly sensitive Ultra intelligence to a Special Liaison Unit (SLU). An SLU officer would personally deliver the Ultra message to the Allied commander in the field, allow him to read and absorb, then destroy it.

No mention was made of Bletchley Park. Cover stories were used, such as 'a reliable source recovered a flimsy bit of a message in the wastepaper basket of ...'. To avoid enemy suspicion that Enigma was being read, information had always to be verified, and reconnaissance aircraft were sometimes sent, merely so they might be spotted by the enemy.

Today Block E houses commercial offices and is not open to the public.

Charts covered the walls for calculations and mapping

Block E was a communications hub

Secrecy was absolute

Typex machines were used to re-encipher outgoing messages

Block F

During World War Two, Block F became the world's first purpose-built computer centre. The Newmanry and the Testery moved in with Colossus, the world's first working electronic computer, invented by engineer Tommy Flowers to speed up the breaking of the fiendishly complex Lorenz cipher. Block F also housed the Japanese codebreaking sections. It was demolished in 1988.

The first Colossus arrived at Bletchley Park in 1944. By the end of the war there were ten. Donald Michie, a member of The Newmanry, said, 'Each one was like a very big wardrobe. It was a scene you didn't see again until about 1960 with huge main-frames, going flat out around the clock.'

Above: Lorenz (aka Tunny) Room

Left: The Testery was housed in Block F

Block H

Block H housed Colossus and Robinson machines. It was completed by June 1944 and occupied by mid-September. By October 1944, Block H was also used to house captured German and Italian cipher equipment and 88 captured machines were stored there.

Today Block H houses The National Museum of Computing.

Above: Colossus

Left: Block H today

People

During World War One Britain built up a significant Signals Intelligence operation, listening to enemy radio traffic. The Government Code & Cypher School (GC&CS) was created at the end of the war and developed over the next two decades. By 1939 veteran cryptanalysts from World War One such as John Tiltman, Dilly Knox, Hugh Foss and Frank Birch, plus linguists and classicists, formed the core of GC&CS's expertise. They were joined by men and women recruited from industry and other branches of academia. This eclectic mix of people, together with the rarefied atmosphere of Bletchley Park and the great sense of its work's importance, made for a unique experience.

The Bletchley Park Recreational Club included a library, drama group, music and choral societies as well as bridge, chess, fencing and Scottish dancing. Wrens drafted in to operate the Bombes were billeted together at local country houses including Woburn Abbey, and the 'Wrenneries' became renowned for their dances.

Rounders on the Lawn

Bletchley Park had a thriving amateur dramatics scene

Skating on the Lake, January 1940

Musical and theatrical productions were popular

Fencing at Bletchley Park

Many romances blossomed here, and numerous couples went on to marry. But they had all signed the Official Secrets Act and kept their vow of silence until the story of what was achieved here began to emerge in the 1970s. Then, and even now, some remain tight-lipped about their part in the codebreaking operation because they had sworn to do so.

Many of the Codebreakers went on to achieve high positions in academia, business and politics after the war. Some played a key role in developing GCHQ, as GC&CS was renamed.

Women made up the majority of the personnel at Bletchley Park, and not only in supporting roles: they made a significant contribution to the codebreaking. The working culture was described by American cryptographer William Friedman as one where 'Rank or status cuts no ice'.

Women outnumbered men at Bletchley Park by around three to one

Restoration

2014 was an exciting landmark year for Bletchley Park. Following 22 years of hard work by the Bletchley Park Trust it saw the completion of the first phase of essential restoration to the World War Two landscape, the iconic codebreaking huts and the transformation of Block C into a vibrant and atmospheric Visitor Centre featuring an interactive introductory exhibition, a coffee shop and a gift shop.

The next phase of the project to restore Bletchley Park is expected to cost in the order of £20 million and take ten years to complete. This will enable the Bletchley Park Trust to restore the remaining historic buildings, currently derelict or not fit for use, and to further develop its educational programme and exhibitions for ever-increasing numbers of visitors.

The Bletchley Park Trust has a responsibility to safeguard this important site for future generations, in permanent and fitting tribute to those extraordinary people who worked here during World War Two, and to tell their stories in the buildings in which they undertook the work that helped change the very course of history.

Introductory Exhibition in the newly restored Block C

The landscape returned to wartime parkland

'The work here at Bletchley Park ... was utterly fundamental to the survival of Britain and to the triumph of the west. I'm not actually sure that I can think of very many other places where I could say something as unequivocal as that. This is sacred ground. If this isn't worth preserving, what is?'

Professor Richard Holmes, Military Historian

On 18 June 2014 Bletchley Park was visited by HRH The Duchess of Cambridge to formally open the newly restored codebreaking Huts 3 and 6, the Visitor Centre in Block C and the transformed landscape.

HRH The Duchess of Cambridge arrives at Bletchley Park

HRH The Duchess of Cambridge meets BP veterans in the newly restored Block C

Bletchley Park Trust Chairman Sir John Scarlett KCMG OBE proudly welcomes HRH The Duchess of Cambridge

Acknowledgements

Wartime images of Bletchley Park: Crown copyright, reproduced with kind permission of the Director, GCHQ. Due to the high level of secrecy surrounding the work carried out at Bletchley Park, relatively few wartime images exist, so images do not necessarily depict the exact buildings or functions being described around them. However, they still indicate the atmosphere and approach to furnishing. Image on p.8 (left) courtesy of Bundesarchiv (Gz: B6-2012/A-2338).

Cover and modern images of Bletchley Park © ShaunArmstrong/mubsta.com.

Thanks go to: English Heritage, in particular Jeremy Lake, GCHQ Historian, Michael Smith, author of The Secrets of Station X, Frank Carter, the Noble family, the Hodsdon family, Bob Horner and Joel Greenberg,

In 2005, English Heritage produced comprehensive reports on the historic value and importance of Bletchley Park. They have become a definitive set of documents which informed this guidebook.

You can find out more from English Heritage at www.english-heritage.org.uk

ISBN 978-1-84165-593-2   6/17
Printed in Turkey.

Pitkin Publishing, Pavilion Books Company Limited
43 Great Ormond Street, London WC1N 3HZ.
www.pavilionbooks.com   +44 (0)20 7462 1506

Memorial designed by Charles Gurrey, unveiled by HM The Queen in July 2011

ENGLISH HERITAGE